KES Private Tu

'Be A Part Of the Solution'

Academics and Students

Need a One to One Specialized Professional Service?
Need Support In achieving Your Grades/Goals?

Start here with Our Professional Study Coach!

Parents with teenagers

Struggling to support Education?
Losing track of their homework and study?
Want to give support, but theres no time?

Start here with Our Study Buddy Service!

Free Consultation & Pre-Assessment

What we offer

- Affordable Prices
- Assigned Personal Teacher
- Proofreading, Punctuation
- Spelling and Grammar
- Reading and Writing
- Follow up
- Support with Assignments

What we Teach

- A Level English
- Basic: ICT
- Basic English
- GCSE English
- Functional Skills: ESOL
- Functional Skills: Literacy
- Entry Level 1-3
- Level 1-2

Check Out Our Website Or Contact Us For Further information

T: 02085344233 M: 07506437221 E: info@kreativeeducationalsolutions.co.uk
W: www.kreativeeducationalsolutions.co.uk   W: www.kespublishing.co.uk

KESPUBLISHING

Professional Writing | Publishing Services

'Our Aim Is To Create Authors Out Of Budding Writers'

Publishing

Free Consultation
Book Cover Design
Book Layout
Editing/Proofing
Distribution Advice & Support
Kindle Formatting

Professional Writing

Proofreading
CV, Cover, Formal Letter Writing
Manuscript Editing/Proofing
Assignment Editing/Proofing
Support, Advice & Guidance
Follow Up Support

'Give A Unique Memorable Gift'

Personalised Poetry
For Spiritual & Special Occasions

Birthday's
Christening's
Communion's
Wedding's
Funeral's
Themed occasion: Leaving work

Contact Us & Check Out KES Website & Amazon For Publications

T :02085344233   M: 07506437221   E :info@kreativeeducationalsolutions.co.uk
W :www.kreativeeducationalsolutions.co.uk   W :www.kespublishing.co.uk

Dedicated

to

*Mama with all my Love
Bertillier Panthier Samuel
AKA Mama
Who lived by her value of a higher power,
support and belief in the importance of family, community
spirit
and*
LAUGHTER

22/12/22 - 29/05/98

Acknowledgement

Kreative Educational Solutions would like to thank the KES staff team and contributors: Antonia Charles, Desta and Reka Samuel, Terri Eze, Janine Rowe-Simpson, Jazante Samuels, Jean Shervington Worrell, Josephine Sedoc, Jordan Constantine, Maureen Ledeatte, Monawara Ali and Nubian-tee.

KES would like to thank all of the individuals and organisations that have supported us in delivering this writing experience to the community. Firstly, our funders The Big Lottery for believing in KES's vision. Additionally the KES Family of volunteers, Shaleta and Jamel Grant, Gary Hutson, the late Maxwell Barrington Grant AKA Ranking Trevor, Cornerstone Trio and Joel Gayle.

Editor: Augustina Samuel
Project Manager: Nubian-tee

KESPublishing

Our mission is to encourage and build the confidence in unpublished writers. Through KESPublishing support we aim to inspire them to reach and obtain their goal of becoming published authors in their own right.

POETIC VOICES

VOICES FROM THE COMMUNITY

Written by Reconnect Through Writing: Writers Group
London, UK.

First published in 2012 in the UK by
KESPublishing
PO Box 68366
London E7 7DG

E-book and hard copy available on website and Amazon
E : as@kespublishing.co.uk
W: http://kreativeducationalsolutions.co.uk
W: http://kespublishing.co.uk

Copyrights in the works contained in this book belongs to the identified contributors. No part of this publication may be reproduced, stored in a retrieval system or transmitted, in any form or by any means, mechanical, photocopying, recording or otherwise, without the prior written permission of both the copyright owners and the publisher of this book.

All rights reserved.

Book Layout and Cover design: Augustina Samuel
Background to Poetic Voices

Poetic Voices is the realization of a life's purpose and dream that began 16 years ago to bring the love of creative writing to my local community and improve reading and writing skills as a result. This has been achieved through the support and funding from the Big Lottery. Creative writing for me is an innate talent you either have it or you do not. However, I do believe that the talent could be unrealised and laid dormant within, unless that talent is unlocked, inspired, nurtured, and guided effectively. Once the talent for sharing words is established there is then a need to learn conventions, forms, style, genre etc. How do you write? why do you write? and ultimately, what do you write? There is then the need to study your art. Hence the need for funding and support of community creative writing projects. Creative writing aids as it is a part of the personal development process as it is organic.

Sharing the love of the word and how it can change lives is immense, books and words bring knowledge and wisdom about life's tests and trials. I have come to believe that the mind, the eyes, the mouth, and the hand are for me the most essential parts of the body. The concept must first be implanted, then visualized, it must be believed in for the concept to manifest. It is then important to act in order to make that concept a reality. However the whole process of communications and the various forms and vehicles it takes as we are used to relay that information can truly be amazing. The nineteenth and twentieth century specifically the latter has been responsible for the most immense technological advancements. Due to these advancements it allows for an individual to have an idea of a dream to produce and publish a book themselves for, by and about the community speaking about the ordinary, everyday issues and struggles that they face daily in their lives. It is through this that the idea of bringing the two creative writing projects Reconnect Through Writing and The Lyrical Camp were born. It demonstrates that there could really be a story hidden away in each of us. This book has something for everyone and mass appeal. Supporting this book you are not just obtaining a book to read, you are indeed supporting the community, education and the unemployed into employment through your participation in this writing experience.

Editor: Augustina Samuel

Table of contents

Background to Poetic Voices: Augustina Samuel
Free: Nubian-tee
To dare: Terri Eze
Words: Jean Shervington-Worrell
Free to be me: Jazante Samuels
Gratitudes are for always: Josephine Sedoc
My bible: Antonia Charles
Dedicated to dad: Maureen Ledeatte
When party did a play: Janine Rowe-Simpson
I remember: Josephine Sedoc
Lesson learnt: Reka Samuel
Lost for words: Reka Samuel
FEAR: Janine Rowe-Simpson
The sock eating monster: Janine Rowe-Simpson
A mothers love: Nubian-tee
What am I: Jordan Constantine
Institutional Oppression: Nubian-tee
Christian Dior: Jean Shervington-Worrell
Original Rasta: Desta Samuel
Transformed: Nubian-tee
Drop in the ocean: Monawara Ali
Thank u T: Jean Shervington-Worrell
Life's Purpose: Nubian-tee
Alive: Terri Eze
Spare the rod and spoil the child: Nubian-tee
Background to contributors: Augustina Samuel
Author Biography: Shaleta Grant

Free
What you've given to me not a fanfare or a jamboree
What you've given to me It's not a party, fantasy nor a great big movie
Almighty God what you've given to me, is the joy and inspiration for us all to be free
To be free creatively
To be free learnedly
To be free with productivity
We've now learnt to sing in harmony
Even wrote a poem called Thank you T

Yes, I want you to know what really inspires me
Is to impart the knowledge that allows other to run free
Words are special
Their innate
Their inborn
God gave me the gift to share and forewarn
To guide, to shape and then to make
I SWEAR to you, i'm not a fake
This dream that I had was just festering in me
Gave me gifts grace and talents, armor sanctified me

Free to knock down the walls that were hidden to me
Free to knock down the doors that I just could not see
Free to knock down the ideas that limited me
Free to knock down the stereotypes that imprisoned me
Free to knock down the barriers set there before me
Free to on knock on the door of spirituality
Free to on knock on the door of sincerity
Free to on knock on the doors of opportunity
Free to hope to dream
To have the faith, dare to be me

Ms Angelou wrote that she was not perfect, but by the grace of God He said she was worth it.
Mr Shakespeare performed, wrote sonnets and plays
That illustrated and discussed love in many different ways
He spoke of love in ways that have been quoted
His opinions and views are dually noted
But none are as eloquent and profound as the one He has written
For He lost it all for us to be forgiven

Baldwin said in, No name in the street
Beware of becoming the victim as you give your power away
Do not be led astray
Live to fight another day
Injustice is wrong, you must stand up and say.

Nubian-tee

To Dare
Dare to stand out and rise above
Be different
Make a name, and find a reason
Dare to ponder, **If**

Dare to dream
Have a vision
And believe, **Only**

Dare to laugh at adversity
Go the distance and be bold,
Take a chance
And think, **You**

Dare to walk the plank
Make your mark
And shape your purpose, **Will**

Dare to be quirky
Be smart, or funny
Find romance,
And to love, **Dare**

Dare to explore, to resist
Convention, and be challenged
And to journey, **To**
Dare to run your race
And hold the banner,
Your destiny
Believe.

Terri Eze

Words

Words are the ultrasound, that echoes are all round
Yes you're spellbound and dumbfound from the penetrating rebounds of sound
A merry-go-round, sometimes feeling giddy as you hit the ground

Words are elements language, casting everlasting contracts of the years long past
Words illustrate and improvise histories great glories and untold stories of

Poverty, wealth, slavery, cruelty, struggle, human rights, civil rights, Prejudice, injustice!!

An outcry and abomination that discrimination coexist
Its the same sound that echoes all around
Bomb bang
The bells are ringing and the birds are singing the sound that echoes
All around

Ta! Ta! Ta!
Da! Da! Da!
Blah! Blah! Blah!

Hit me with your rhythm stick oh! words of sound
Listen to the beat of the drums
Hounding and surrounding the ground that pounds

the words of Simplicity, honesty, sincerity, truthfulness, openness, authenticity, Legality, Integrity

JUSTICE!!!

Listen and in time you will hear and understand echoing all around.

Jean Shervington-Worrell

Free just to be me

Black, red
Up and down
Inside out
Confused, really confused.
Different people having their feuds
No time to stop and be renewed
Changing swaying, scrambling praying,
When will it be time, to be just me?

Now and then
Or when you choose
Please, please I scream don't let me be used
Do this they say, do that, they say
Move it, fetch it, so much abuse

I do not choose
No, you do
But it's not me
Why an earth can't you see
This way and that way, with no release
Let me be!!!

Lonely and afraid to stand up for myself
It's always in vain
I just can't wait to get out of this day,
I can then choose to be me another day, in a different way

Your reality is not my reality
Your thoughts are your thoughts
My thoughts are my own

Squeeze me, condense me into your pigeon feed
Toss me, turn me, expect me to squeal
Hurt me at will, you will never control
My will is my will
God knows you can not tame
Strong and courageous,
Sexy, if I choose
Successful and powerful
Changing all the rules to make history
Helping those like me
Trying so hard, just to be free
So very free, just to be me.

Jazante Samuels

Gratitude is for Always

No matter who you are
No matter where you are
Gratitude can dissolve all negativity in your life
No matter what form it has taken.

The Secret Gratitude book
I wake up, what am I grateful for today?
I have life, I can breathe, see, speak, listen
Move into my being
God's Spirit is alive in me
I am grateful.

I have this new day to begin again. To live good, to do right, to give love to all whom I meet
I am grateful.

Every day I aim high to make a difference in this world through all my thoughts, words and deeds, it give me joy to do so. I am grateful.

My loved ones are blessed with life, health and are safe in God's care each day. I am grateful
I am so blessed each day to know that the universe is on my side faithfully guiding my way through this life
What am I grateful for. Everything.

However big however small the blessings are
Father God Almighty
Thank you for them all.

Josephine Sedoc

My Bible

The bible I have come to think
Could have been written by the spirits,
It is very holy
And should only be read slowly
Do we stop to think
What this thing really is?
Do we understand?
The Psalms whilst we hold it in our palms.

I love this book whilst I stop to look
Focusing on its pages
Analysing the stages
Hollywood retold the stories
Cleopatra, Samson and Moses
But Proverbs I find engages you
From an excellent point of view
Matthew is a thorough verse
And the other's tells many parables.

Genesis highlights the beginning
But that's dependent upon whose reading
Once you get this book
it might just give you the hook
To guide your life
Out of trouble and strife
Allow your participation
In living a peaceful life.

Antonia Charles

Dedicated to Dad

Thank you for agreeing to be my Dad
Thank you for making me extremely glad
That I came into this life to express and be free
And experience life for what it really could be.

Thank you for the way we were grown
Exposure to music, opportunities were shown
With the freedom to explore
Life really couldn't be a bore.

Four offspring, Oh what a delight
The photo you took of us to be constant in sight
So quietly proud, unique and creative
You inspired us to be embracing and supportive.

Our brother so pleased as punch
The rest of the family, a happy bunch
To see you at long last leave that box of fear
When you decided to take to the air.

Unable to celebrate your 50th with pride
With mum your childhood sweetheart by your side
Either on your dream cruise or in your mini cooper
We celebrate your life as a trouper.
When I imagine you jamming with James Brown
Getting on the good foot, I can't wear a frown
The greatest lesson that you have taught
Is that time is of the essence and can't be bought.
To the only father I once had here on earth
Now with two in heaven, I look forward to my rebirth.

Maureen Ledeatte

When party did a play

Remember back in the day, when party did a play
when mummy and daddy would dance the night away

When we would sit on the stairs with eyes open wide
when big people would look at us
we would run and hide

When Babycham and Cherry B was big people tipple
When no one was looking we teef a lickle
But if we were lucky
Mummy and Daddy would give us a lickle

Oh, Curry Goat and Rice did cook in da kitchen
those days were great and life seemed sweet
Just thinking of those days makes me curl up me feet.

Janine Rowe-Simpson

I Remember

I remember when as a girl When I was young
We played safely on the streets
And each neighbor knew everyone.

I remember the hot summer days
When as friends of colour together
To the park we would go and play.

I remember the young respected the old,
Rudeness and bad attitude
What was that? You could never be so bold.

I remember people fought with their fists,
Nowadays guns and knives, my God
Has it really come to this?

I remember the music I listened to was all
Love and romance.
Now the young only rap about killing
And life is only a chance.

I remember, I remember.

Josephine Sedoc

Lesson Learnt?

Born into a world of patriarchy and capitalism
Where LABELING of individuals depict the future we see them in.
Us, young youths following the typecast
Behaving insubordinate, portraying the image of the working class.

Looking through the mirror of our own reflection
All that stares back is a face full of confusion
There stands a young black female with ambition piercing through her eyes.
Her intelligence and potential
All covered up with lies
The lies that make her steal
The lies that make her gloat
The lies that slowly take away all her chances of hope.

She's kinda lost, you know, kinda confused
There goes another lost friend of hers headlined on the 6 o'clock news
Stood in turmoil, stuck at a crossroads, there leads the the right path
She takes the wrong turn
And that voice inside her head continues to scream
"WHEN WILL YOU EVER LEARN?"
Is this not extreme!

Day by day, hour by hour
The mentality of youths these days grow vicious and harsher.
Girls pregnant by age of 16
Question, "who's the father?"

Boys in and out of jail, crime rates increasing ever further.

Old people always say "well back in my day"
Don't you think it will be interesting to hear what our generation will have to say
Youth these days have taken a violent turn
And again I repeat
When will they ever learn.

Reka Samuel

Lost for words

I gained a little but I lost a lot
Yeah my family says that i lost the plot
Can't think straight
No
My minds a blur
Look to the sky to pray
But can't find the words
To even, say
Visions in my mind
Of what is, meant to be
Things are so different, in reality
So I pray again
But yet still I get no reply
Nothing changes around me
Is religion a lie?
You look at me
And think I don't try
But the truth you'll find
Lies into my eyes
Where you see the fear
And see there's no becoming myself
Again.

Reka Samuel

Fear

Sometimes pain that's been inflicted takes time to erode
Old dark shadows etched into cells of our DNA

Tucked away in our memories like skin layers
Carrying century old stigma's and dogma
Representing unjust laws of evil men

But we were never as described
we were always strong and bold
full of wisdom and knowledge from old
there is no period, no full stop, where the light has not shone
from the beginning of life's dark creation.

The Sock Eating Monster

I know there is a sock eating monster
What! you may exclaim,
What! I did not stutter and no I don't know its name
All I know is that this monster does not like pairs,
And it seems invisible as you never know if it is there.

However, if you do not pair those socks, you must weep for them as lost.
Do not bother trying to find them, oh no, not at any cost.

Janine Rowe-Simpson

What I am ?
Is it the yellow paint that's been permanently smeared on my skin?
Or is it the fact that I'm not a whole breed?
Is it the curls in my hair, or the colour of my eyes?
Or is the fact that my white father implanted into my black mother?
His reproductive seed?
Is it the shape of my body that defines both sides of me?
Or is it the fact that I'm lighter and darker than either side of me?

The questions and a sense of dark impurity
Flow around my ghostly spirit, with a haunting laugher that's etched inside of me
The dark shadows of the truth or what I am and what I'll be.
Lay waiting in the dark, ready to pounce on me.

This insecurity of the colour of my skin has left its scar on me
Like a tagged eagle in the air, so much distance but many boundaries
I was once proud of what I am, but I've seen the world as it should never be
A dark and mystifying creation where the Devil has left his dirty seed.

Mixed race is the combination of two colours
Created by pure genetics and the love of others
But, how we first came about was not out of love
It was the greed and sexual desires of a lustful little bug.

Where the foundation of my race was built.
Was on a ship from the mother land to a nation on stilts.
This fake power that they thought they could embed
This rule that one was superior to the other was etched within our heads.
How this, dirty, promiscuous, egotistical race of mine appeared. By the way that's what we are now seen by others.
Happened many years ago
When one side of me raped the other.

How can I be proud of something so disgusting?
There was no love in the creation of what I am.
Nowadays the girls that are mixed race,
Are now the ones that are least trusted

Mixed race girls get called skets and slags
They're always getting accused of being with different mans
How we cant stay faithful or loyal to even one
How we're always in bed with Michael, Harry, Peter, and even John
It's like we're all living in a world inside of a world

To and fro, discrimination is always being hurled
There's whites, and coloureds and then the confused lot
Soon the fact that we are black and white will surely be forgot.

I don't want to deny any side of me
But it seems that way
Seeing as I have been brought up in black family
Technically, there's no white in me.

My mother told me to never deny the white side
But it's hard though, when I'm living a lie
I don't feel like I'm a white child
My heart tells me I am a black child.

But it doesn't matter what I feel
It's how the world sees me that's all that matters
I am just a yellow speck with curly hair
My existence doesn't seem to matter.

I am a white man's and a black woman's daughter
One eye witnessed the process of my ancestors slaughter.

Whilst the other eye witnesses us basking in glory
That they could live to tell the white supreme story
I've now come to realise that I am unique
I no longer care about the jealous remarks made.

I am a black and white child
For a special reason I was born this way.

I will never really understand who I am
But what I am I know for sure
My name is *Jordan Nicole Andie Constantine*
I am a yellow child, I don't really care anymore.

Jordan Constantine

Institutional Oppression

Towering over me with a pillar of strength
He represents the establishment
And all that I resent
You're an aberration
Why are you seeking an education?
Know your place, young girl!
Get back to your station.

Nubian intimidation
Black prowess
Pouncing on our
Snow White innocence
Quiet, but dominate
Subtle, yet violent
Know your history, young girl
Check your ancestry.

Condescendingly
He stamps his authority
Trying to undermine me
Preaching his superiority
Expressing all his bigotry
To show my inferiority.

But, strong was I born
And all before
Proud was I born
And all before
Innovative was I born
And all before

Respect is due, i'm telling you
Don't wanna dismiss you, I have already forgiven you
I serve one higher, that is stronger than you
I am not beholden to you
And I mean it, true.

Disrespect, i'll still come correct
The power that is mine, I will protect
I'm trying to live a life that I won't regret
The blessing of the Lord, I will beset
Peace be unto you, i'll just say bless you
The salvation i've been graced with, you can't deny.

The angels are around me watch me soar and fly
I'm blessed with Him around me
I can testify
He'll wrap in his love
On Him I will rely.

Nubian-tee

Christian Dior

It's a puzzle and I am muzzled without sound
And as I look around I see the flickering light

It reminds me of the time I got sight of Mama bickering at the sickening thought that Gracie had bought a cat that messed on the mat and sat on she good hat.

Get out you brat of a cat, Gracie, were you born a twat? Mama would say, oh I pray for the day when ya'all will understand or should I write it in longhand that strays are not allowed in the house, only if it catch a mouse.

Gracie was always in a rubble, Ahh! she just attract trouble. And Mama always mad with she, especially when she pour Mama Christian Dior in the sink
She just don't think, it would link Mama to the brink, of hitting she with the broom and locking she in she room.
Quietly, I sit outside Gracie room, I sing a melody so she know and see, i'm not mad with she.
Oh Mama show compassion, she learn she lesson, don't put Gracie in isolation and condemnation, she needs motivation not depravation.

Does Mama hear, all she think bout is she Christian Dior she have no more.

Jean Shervington-Worrell

A Mothers Love

Stop the violence
We need more peace
We'll no longer stand in silence
The war must cease

Why are you killing, stabbing and hurting your fellow brother?
Why do you hurt the heart of your mother?
Were you not taught to love one and another?
Brotherly and sisterly love
We need to endeavour

Nine months to carry
Now its time to bury
Another life wasted
Unable to fulfil His purpose
You're a victim to surplus
You're just worthless

Lockdown now you see what life was meant to be
The endless possibilities
You're worth it
Knowledge is wisdom
Wisdom is education
Education is the key

Unlock your gifts and talents
You're special
You're unique
You're classic
Be an example to follow
Don't just passively eat up and swallow
There is a time to follow there is a time to lead
Make sure your steadfast in the time of need

Guns, knives, bottles bricks
What's that rhyme about bones and sticks?
They said words will never hurt cha
Yes they can, and also nurture
Me all my life
Learn how words can bring you love, calm and also peace
Spiritual Scripture empowerment led
Words and words fill my head
Never be a Simon Said

The gate is now open step up and try
Go on and stride
Reach, love, deep inside
Write, achieve and you will learn
Then you'll know, you will earn
Growth through
Lessons learnt.

Nubian-tee

Original Rasta

Original Rasta, know that I trust yah, In everything you do and
Say I ras-pect yah, no fool can dis yah, or take the piss nah
Cause you come with original, roots & culture
You ban dem vulture, and gal dat love murder
Sodom and Gomorra get bun inna
Bingi, fire, i'm feeling your skin, your a carbon
Essence of boundless blackness

Your the latest
Love how you dress
Your more than less
Your a black diamond inna
Pool of black pearls
Me forsake you, no, never
Cause i'd never be whole without yah
With Ras i'm falling deeper
True His knowledge, and knowledge is power
Teach the youths, to fight for their rights
Divine pillar, never a killer it's not in his nature

Eat pork, no never, no, Your a veggie, vegan member
No pretender, no, never, Stick to your princibles,
even though, they try to break your soul, know, invincible
The pinnacle, damn irresistible
To make love, to you, on a, spiritual level
I'd sell my soul to the devil
You educate my mental, Your fundamental to my survival
There's no rival, that's why they idolize you,
in so many ways

Its unbelievable, inconceivable, peace,to your, spiritual
On a level

Original, brown, ebony skin, your just the one, that I
Need to get in, more than a, blessing, never me ever
Trade you in.
Cause your melanin got me bugging, lethal injecting
E-recting emotions, close to the forces of oceans
That will cover mountains like Jaro, and
Flood the deserts Cairo
You got me drunk up like a wino
Your all that I know,
And I refuse to let you, go, that's why I
Got to praise Him, praise Him.

Desta Samuel

Transformed

Heart wrenching a soldier on the battlefield of existence
Fighting for justice
Just to find a better way of life
I plea, abduct me from this strife
Drug dealer, cleaner, care giver, cook
Transformed to teacher cleansed begin a fresh chapter
Rewrite that book
Drug dealer, cleaner, care giver, cook
Transformed to teacher yeah I like that look

Rescued from hurt yet drowning in sorrow
Oh Lord I pray for my children tomorrow
Pricked by the arrow of despair
Summoned to count out all your wares

Prickling despair
Summoned to account
Doctored by care
And healed by love
Made whole through your devotion
And the knowledge of above

In the garden of life there is no fear
Loneliness is omitted there
Just peace and tranquillity
Reign and triumph here
Surrounded in serenity
Guided by the Holy Trinity
Oh how I know your love for me

The impact of the realisation just hit me
Feed your soul and your spirit will be free
Trust and rejoice in the
Power of the Almighty!

Nubian-tee

Drop in the Ocean

You have to love yourself
Then other's too will love you
Allow yourself to be authentic
Know your essence, your spirit.

Learn to love others unconditionally
Some teach that we are all one
We are all connected but separate.

So by hating another
You are hating part of yourself
Look at the ocean
Some of the water evaporates,
it turns into clouds in the sky
It travels over land and sea
And drops as rain either back in the same ocean
Or several hundred miles away.

But despite it changing form, it is still water
That was once a part of a whole ocean
We are also made up of that ocean
A large percentage of us IS water
We are made from the same essence
When we die we return back to that essence
So You, Me and Everyone
Are made of the same thing
We are ONE!

Monawara Ali

Thank U "T"

I still wonder and certainly ponder how this has come to past
And I am sure this encounter is definitely going to last
Meeting with a sister who was not seen for years
But when we met my eyes was full of happy tears

Yes, "T" what you've done for me is put the honey in my tea
The group's spirit has been uplifted to be creative and its shows that they are all so gifted
What we've all gained, and I am sure the group would say the same,
That "T" has enhanced our skills which give us the thrills to express the inner abilities
To create intensifying stories about our heart-warming woes and glees.

Thanks "T" for the opportunity which has given us the dignity and the undeniable unity
The contributions you've offered the group has tightened the loop and opened the gates of chances which dances and prances along the floor, as it pours different dimensions for our future creations in writing stories of glory, woe and glee.

Jean Shervington-Worrell

Life's Purpose

I was put here to teach
Praise, guide and reach
Those that may seek
To elevate to their peak
In the knowledge of the meek
Hide and don't peek

I have done often thought
To find out, why it may be as it ought
As I have been taught
That goodness is the way
Bend down and obey

Epistemology, left here since eternity
It's all up to you
Now follow the rules

He held my hand and walked me through
The darkness until I came to you
Compelled me to begin a new

So come as you are from near and from far
Come with your scars
He'll make you a star

You will be told, stories old
With characters both young and bold
In your life you may then unfold
To guide you in the way that you should live
With love, that you should always endeavour to give.

Nubian-tee

Alive

Oh, to grasp the time, the moment, the second, the thought. The laughter in ones eye.
The inspiration, the pain, the glory
The sensations the anger, the burning desire
To be, or not to be
The tension, the frustration
To touch the sky, to touch the moon
To feel the victory in ones hands
The glory, the thunder
The river, the rain, the moon, the sun, stars, trees, birds and bees
Oh sweetness, the touch of summer
To come, to go, to dance, to be or not to be
To sigh, to moan losing the moment, the time
The chance
Living, laughter, crying, weeping and moaning
To live, to die, to live to be
This is the time and this is the moment.

Terri Eze

Spare the rod and spoil the child

There was once a couple named Masculine & Ramón and they lived in a place called Dominica located in the West Indies. They could only be described as childhood sweethearts. They had known and grown up with each other since Masculine was aged nine and Ramón was ten years old. Their love for each other was envied by all in the town where they lived. The women folk would be jealous of the way that he would be tentative and gentle with her. In contrast the men would be jealous because he had a woman that doted on him and took care of him they had a kind of undoubting, resolute and reassuring love.

They grew up and at the tender age of 18 years old they decided to get married. It was not a shock to anyone as it had always been expected by the villagers and towns people. Her mother sold fish in the market and her father was a butcher slaughtering and selling meat for a living which in those days was a good thriving profession to be in. let's face it, you always need to eat. His father was a jewellery maker and he fashioned gold into the most exquisite sort after pieces. His mother did not work as there was no need to because she came from a well to do family who were in banking thus they were financially stable. Therefore she had a privileged up bringing.

They were married and it seemed the whole town turned out for the wedding ceremony. One of those occasions that would be marked and spoken about for all time. Her father slaughtered 30 goats and 20 chickens for the ceremony. There was enough food and drink for all until their bellies were so stuffed full that they could not eat another morsel. He became a teacher due to the advantage of being able to afford an education and his wife decided to dedicate herself to the raring of the children the soon to be conceive.

Time passed and people began to talk and whisper as they would pass. "What wrong wid dem, she must be baron; people would comment and ask what they were waiting for. It had been 10 years and still they had not been able to conceive a child. They were God fearing people and that is how they lived. They prayed regularly and consistently to the Father for a child. Although there were times that they felt a little disheartened as they knew that their God was a loving God and as the scriptures state ask and it will be given unto you. They believed that there was a lesson that had to be learnt and when the time was right just as Abraham & Sarah who conceived in their eighties God can and does work miracles. Another 10 years passed and after seeing all number of specialists. Masculine conceived at 38 years of age. it was hailed as a blessing from above by all.

This was the fairytale completed and the knowledge that this was the testament from their faithful unchanging belief and trust in the Lord God. The child was born and it was a son they named him the strong biblical name Issachar meaning: God has given me my reward the same name is also from one of the twelve tribes of Israel. This child grew and became spoilt as they had waited so long for a child they felt unable to say no to him. Consequently, he invariably got whatever he asked for. The towns' people knew him and his bad side but only his parent could not or would not see it.

As a child he would bully and hurt the other children in the town and when their parents would come to Masculine and Ramón for him to be punished and disciplined. The response was always not my child you must be mistaken. It is a sad state when a parent does not know their own child's capabilities. Time went on and he would steal, rob, he even raped a girl in town when he was 18 years old and still the parents said not my child. Money brings power and power brings control. Due to the power the family maintained his crimes would always go unpunished.

One fateful day he had gone into town and got into an argument with the girls family who he had raped. He looked into her brothers eyes and exclaimed you can not touch me, say what you will. A fight ensued and by the end of it the victim's brother lay dead. The fight took place in full view of all the towns' folk. He took up a piece of timber and struck him across the head violently, he fell and lost consciousness, later he stopped breathing. He was pronounced dead on arrival to the hospital.

There was no way to shield him this time, his card had been marked and there were enough witnesses ready willing and prepared to come forward to testify to what they had seen. He was arrested a court case followed and as he was bang to rights, found guilty and he was received the death penalty. The law is a life for a life. He was now in the prison cell awaiting his fate and he was asked what he would like for the last rites before your sentence is carried out. He said he would like to see his mother and he would like a feast with good old caribbean cuisine of steam fish with okra, pumpkin, thyme, carrots spiced up with and rice and kidney beans cooked in coconut cream with a salad side and washed down with a bottle of Dragon Stout. He ate it and it was so delicious for a while he was able to forget his impending doom. Up until that moment he felt the sentence was unjust and he began to pray hysterically crying. But almost in an instant he calmed himself and became still. He prayed for forgiveness and peace and almost miraculously it seemed he had received it and he was ready to meet his maker. He was in a state of kenosis.

The guard came marching to the cell door and shouted "visitor" he jumped up and said let her in. His mother was frantically crying and shouting "why, why, why Lord, was I not faithful enough why do you take my child, my one son, my only child. She was so engulfed in her own misery and sorrow that she did not even notice that her son was just calmly sitting on the edge of the bed as if he had come to terms with his fate and was waiting for her to do the same.

He then turned to her and said mother come over here please. She scurried over to him wiping the tears as they streamed down her face. He said lean forward I want to whisper a message in your ear. He viciously wrapped his lips around his mothers ear, held her firm and as she shrieked, screamed and struggled to become free, he bit her ear off and with a mouth full of blood he spat out her ear. Then he said. Mother if all the time when I was doing wrong you had disciplined and reprimanded me I would not be here today.

The bible says: Spare the rod and spoil the child

There are many parents in today's society who believe to say no to their child is depriving them in some way and it actually hurts too much to say no because they want to give them everything they can or did not have. To parent is the hardest job in the world and as the saying goes, sometimes you need to be cruel to be kind. In this world a child needs to learn that you can not always have what you want and there are reasons for that.

Nubian-tee

Background of contributors
Nubian-tee is a Writer, Essayist and Poet. She also has a BA Honours in Communication/Media Studies and is an independent business woman. She has been writing for years and is currently completing a novel.Teri Eza: Is a Writer, Essayist, Photographer and SENCO specialist. She has a BA Honours in Communications Studies/ Media and is an independent business women. Is currently completing a novel book. Reka Samuel: Currently attends Barking Abbey Sixth Form College and is n her final year studying her A Levels in English, Media and Sociology and will progress on to Brunel University to study for a BA Honours in Media/Communications in 2012.Jordan Constantine: Attends Oak Park Sixth Form and is studying her A Levels in Drama and English among other subject areas. Maureen Ledeatte is a self employed Holistic Therapist and runs workshops in Colour therapy. Monawara Ali is a mother and part time trainer and life Coach. Jazante Samuels works supporting SENCO and also works providing Hoarding Clearance Services. Antonia Charles Is a Secretary and Part time Care Worker in her community. Josephine Sedoc is a specialist in extensive educational support and is currently in Alternative Provisional Education. Janine Rowe-Simpson is a full time carer with ten years of work experience in the social sector in various roles such as Residential Social Worker. Jean Shervington-Worrell has a BA Honours in Social Sciences, Specialist in Management: Areas are Sport and Health. Shaleta Grant is the author of the biography is a BA Honours in Business and Finance and works as a Finance and Human Resources Expert and Consultant. She is a singer song writer and runs singing workshops in her local community.

Augustina Samuel writes under the pseudo name of Nubian-tee and is the editor, publisher, writer and the inspiration behind this book. She has a zeal for promoting and encouraging the enjoyment of reading and writing for pleasure as she believes that it is one of the ingredients needed to raise literacy standards. She has been writing for years and is an educationalist with a passion. She is an Educational Consultant, Teacher, Trainer and Motivational Speaker among numerous and varied vocations which she undertakes, empowering individuals to better their lives and life chances through education both informal, formal and through utilising life experience. Her areas of specialisms are: Education, English, ESOL, Behavioural Management and Business Consultancy. She has over 20 years of work experience in teaching and education as well as the social sector.

Shaleta Grant

'WHO HATH believed our report?
and to whom is the arm of the Lord revealed?'

Isaiah 53: 1